SPACE DOCTRINE PUBLICATION 2-0

INTELLIGENCE

DOCTRINE FOR SPACE FORCES

UNITED STATES SPACE FORCE

NIMBLE BOOKS LLC: THE AI LAB FOR BOOK-LOVERS
~FRED ZIMMERMAN, EDITOR~

Humans and AI making books richer, more diverse, and more surprising.

PUBLISHING INFORMATION

(c) 2023 Nimble Books LLC
ISBN: 978-1-60888-212-0

AI-GENERATED KEYWORD PHRASES

Space Doctrine Publication 2-0; Intelligence; United States Space Force (USSF); intelligence operations; role of intelligence; decision advantage; commanders; levels of intelligence; decision-making; space operational environment; continuous coverage; situational understanding; structure and organizations; space intelligence; relationships and partnerships; Intelligence Community (IC); intelligence disciplines; intelligence process; IPOE; collaboration and partnerships; space operations; acquisition activities; testing activities; definitions; references; resources; space operations.

FRONT MATTER

ABSTRACTS

TL;DR (ONE WORD)

Intelligence.

EXPLAIN IT TO ME LIKE I'M FIVE YEARS OLD

This document is a guide for the United States Space Force on how to gather information and use it to make good decisions. It talks about different levels of information and how they help commanders make choices. It's important to always have information about what's happening in space. The document also talks about the different groups and organizations that work together to gather information and the different ways they do it. It explains that there are different types of information and how they help us understand what's going on in space. It

TL;DR (VANILLA)

This document provides guidance and doctrine for intelligence operations in the United States Space Force. It discusses the role of intelligence in space operations, different levels of intelligence, and the importance of continuous coverage and situational understanding. It also highlights the structure, organizations, relationships, and partnerships involved in space intelligence. The document emphasizes collaboration and partnerships in intelligence operations and its support to space operations, acquisition, and testing activities.

SCIENTIFIC STYLE

This document serves as a guidance and doctrine for intelligence operations within the United States Space Force (USSF). It outlines the role of intelligence in space operations and its contribution to achieving decision advantage. The document discusses the different levels of intelligence and their support in decision-making at various levels. It emphasizes the importance of continuous coverage and situational understanding in the space operational environment. The document provides information on the structure, organizations, relationships, and partnerships within the Intelligence Community (IC) involved in space intelligence. It also covers the various intelligence disciplines and the intelligence process, including IPOE. Collaboration and partnerships are highlighted as essential elements of intelligence operations, and the document emphasizes the role of intelligence in supporting space operations, acquisition, and testing activities. Definitions, references, and resources related to intelligence and space operations are also provided.

ACTION ITEMS

Review and familiarize oneself with the contents of Space Doctrine Publication 2-0, Intelligence.

Identify any areas of interest or relevance to one's own role or responsibilities within the United States Space Force.

Consider how the guidance and doctrine outlined in the document can be applied to enhance intelligence operations and decision-making within the space domain.

Share relevant sections or key takeaways from the document with colleagues or superiors to promote awareness and understanding of the role of intelligence in space operations.

Identify any gaps or areas for improvement in current intelligence practices or processes and propose potential solutions or recommendations based on the analysis.

Figure 1. The AI-generated prompt was: Create a black and white illustration that captures the mood of introspection and determination. The image should convey a sense of focus and strategic thinking, with elements that symbolize the world of intelligence and space operations.

Viewpoints

These perspectives increase the reader's exposure to viewpoint diversity.

Grounds for Dissent

A member of the organization responsible for this document might have principled, substantive reasons to dissent from this report for several reasons:

Overemphasis on military dominance: The document may be perceived as overly focused on achieving decision advantage and military dominance in space operations. A dissenting member may argue that this approach neglects the potential for peaceful cooperation and the exploration of space for non-military purposes, such as scientific research or international collaboration.

Lack of consideration for ethical implications: The document may not sufficiently address the ethical implications of intelligence operations in space. A dissenting member may argue that there should be clear guidelines and limitations in place to ensure that intelligence activities are conducted ethically and do not violate human rights or privacy.

Insufficient emphasis on transparency and accountability: The document may not adequately emphasize the importance of transparency and accountability in space intelligence operations. A dissenting member may argue that there should be mechanisms in place to ensure public oversight and to prevent abuses of power within intelligence organizations.

Inadequate acknowledgment of environmental impact: The document may not adequately address the potential environmental impact of space intelligence operations. A dissenting member may argue that there should be a greater focus on minimizing the ecological footprint of intelligence activities in space, such as reducing space debris or mitigating the effects of satellite launches on the Earth's atmosphere.

Neglect of diplomatic and peaceful resolution: The document may overlook the potential for diplomatic and peaceful resolution of conflicts in space. A dissenting member may argue that intelligence operations should be seen as a supporting tool for diplomacy rather than solely focusing on military strategies.

Underrepresentation of diverse perspectives: The document may not adequately consider the diverse perspectives and expertise within the intelligence community. A dissenting member may argue that there should be more inclusion of different viewpoints to ensure a comprehensive and well-rounded understanding of space intelligence operations.

Overall, these dissenting views highlight the importance of considering ethical, environmental, diplomatic, and inclusive perspectives in space intelligence operations. They advocate for a more balanced approach that takes into account the broader implications and potential consequences of intelligence activities in space.

Red Team Critique

The document, titled "Space Doctrine Publication 2-0, Intelligence," provides a comprehensive overview of the role and importance of intelligence in United States Space Force (USSF) operations. It effectively outlines the various levels of intelligence and their contribution to decision-making at different levels. The emphasis on continuous coverage and situational understanding in the space operational environment is commendable.

One area that could be improved in the document is the discussion of the structure and organizations involved in space intelligence. While it briefly mentions these aspects, it would benefit from providing more in-depth information on the specific roles and responsibilities of each organization. This would provide readers with a clearer understanding of the overall framework of space intelligence operations.

Additionally, the document briefly mentions the relationships and partnerships within the Intelligence Community (IC) but does not delve into details about how these partnerships are fostered or maintained. Expanding on this aspect would give readers a better understanding of the collaborative nature of intelligence operations and the importance of sharing information and resources across agencies.

While the document discusses the various intelligence disciplines and the intelligence process, it lacks specific examples or case studies to illustrate these concepts. Including real-world scenarios would make the content more relatable and help readers grasp the practical application of intelligence in space operations.

Furthermore, the document could benefit from a more explicit discussion on the challenges and limitations of intelligence in the space domain. By acknowledging potential constraints, such as limited satellite coverage or the difficulty of monitoring activities in deep space, the document would provide a more well-rounded perspective on the capabilities and constraints of space intelligence.

Lastly, although the document highlights the role of intelligence in supporting space operations, acquisition, and testing activities, it could be strengthened by providing more specific examples or case studies of intelligence contributions in these areas. This would demonstrate the tangible impact of intelligence in enhancing space operations and inform readers of the potential benefits of leveraging intelligence capabilities.

Overall, the document provides a solid foundation for understanding the role of intelligence in USSF operations. By addressing the areas mentioned above and incorporating additional examples and case studies, it would enhance the comprehensiveness and practicality of the content.

MAGA PERSPECTIVE

This document is just another example of the deep state's control over our military. The United States Space Force (USSF) should be focused on defending our country and not wasting resources on intelligence operations in space. This is nothing more than a continuation of the failed policies of the Obama administration.

Why do we need continuous coverage and situational understanding in space? We should be putting America first, not worrying about what other countries are doing up there. Our priority should be protecting American interests and ensuring the security of our nation, not gathering intel on other countries' space activities.

The fact that this document emphasizes collaboration and partnerships with the Intelligence Community (IC) is concerning. We've seen time and time again how the IC has been corrupted by partisan politics. We cannot trust them to provide unbiased and accurate intelligence. The Space Force should be independent and free from these influences.

Additionally, the reference to the intelligence disciplines and process, including IPOE, is another example of bureaucratic jargon that has no place in our military. We need a streamlined and efficient force, not more layers of unnecessary complexity.

Lastly, it is unacceptable that this document provides definitions, references, and resources related to intelligence and space operations. It's time for the Space Force to focus on its core mission and not get bogged down in the minutiae of intelligence gathering. This document is a waste of taxpayer dollars and does nothing to advance the interests of the American people.

SUMMARIES

1   Space Doctrine Publication 2-0, Intelligence, published by STARCOM in July 2023, provides guidance and information on intelligence operations in the context of space.

2   SDP 2-0, Intelligence establishes doctrine for USSF intelligence operations in space, emphasizing the importance of intelligence and the role of Guardians. It provides guidance for decision-making and strategy development, incorporating lessons learned and validated concepts. The publication is authoritative and encourages study and learning.

3   This page is the table of contents for Space Doctrine Publication 2-0, Intelligence. It covers topics such as the role of intelligence in space operations, intelligence disciplines, the intelligence process, and intelligence organizations and relationships.

4   Space Doctrine Publication 2-0 provides guidance for the proper use of military spacepower, establishing principles and guidance for decision-making. It is part of the Space Force doctrine hierarchy, which includes capstone, keystone, operational, and tactical levels. SDP 2-0 specifically focuses on intelligence operations in support of space operations.

5   Space Doctrine Publication 2-0, Intelligence, discusses the role of intelligence in military spacepower and its integration with other disciplines. It also covers joint intelligence disciplines, the intelligence process, and Space Force organizations supporting intelligence efforts.

6   This page discusses the importance of timely and accurate intelligence in achieving decision advantage for commanders in the space domain. It outlines the role of Guardians in providing intelligence, surveillance, and reconnaissance (ISR) as part of the joint force. The page also highlights the Space Force's ability to deliver military spacepower and its cornerstone responsibilities.

7   This page discusses the concept of competition in space operations and the role of intelligence in supporting these operations. It highlights the need to understand adversary capabilities, intentions, vulnerabilities, and readiness in order to gain a decision advantage. The page also includes examples of space intelligence operations.

8   Intelligence is crucial in the space operations environment, helping commanders understand and prioritize activities, allocate resources, and make better decisions. The space operational environment is multi-domain, involving operations in various domains and spectrum environments.

9   The page discusses the role of intelligence in space operations, including its importance in decision-making, resource allocation, and risk assessment. It also explains the three levels of intelligence (strategic, operational, and tactical) and how they inform different levels of command. Additionally, it highlights the integration of intelligence into the spacepower disciplines.

10   This page discusses the various disciplines within space warfare, including orbital warfare, space electromagnetic warfare, space battle management, space access and sustainment, and engineering and acquisition. It

emphasizes the importance of intelligence analysis in informing decision-making and maintaining freedom of action in the space domain.

NOTABLE PASSAGES

1   "Intelligence is a critical component of space operations, providing
     commanders with the necessary information and analysis to make
     informed decisions. It encompasses the collection, processing, analysis,
     and dissemination of information about potential adversaries, the space
     environment, and friendly forces. The intelligence process involves the
     systematic gathering and evaluation of data from a variety of sources,
     including satellites, ground-based sensors, human intelligence, and open-
     source information. This information is then analyzed and synthesized to
     produce actionable intelligence that supports mission planning, threat
     assessment, and operational decision-making. Effective intelligence enables
     commanders to understand the capabilities and intentions of potential
     adversaries, anticipate threats, and exploit opportunities. It also facilitates
     the protection of friendly forces and assets, enhances situational
     awareness, and enables effective targeting and employment of space
     capabilities. In an increasingly contested and congested space domain,
     intelligence is vital for maintaining superiority and achieving mission
     success."

2   "Space Doctrine Publication (SDP) 2-0, Intelligence establishes doctrine
     for United States Space Force (USSF) intelligence operations to support
     the freedom to operate in, from, and to space."

4   "Space Force doctrine guides the proper use of military spacepower in
     support of the Service's cornerstone responsibilities. It establishes a
     common framework for employing Guardians as part of a broader joint
     force. Doctrine provides fundamental principles and authoritative guidance
     for the employment of military spacepower and an informed starting point
     for decision-making and strategy development."

5   "Chapter 5 presents Space Force organizations supporting intelligence,
     and how space is engaged across the Intelligence Community (IC), and
     with other organizations, agencies, allies, and partners to source
     intelligence data in support of joint and combined operations."

6   "Timely and accurate intelligence is essential in achieving decision
     advantage for commanders at every echelon. Intelligence is one of the
     spacepower disciplines in which Guardians specialize, providing data and
     information essential to operations in the space domain, in areas of
     responsibility in every other domain, and in the information and
     electromagnetic spectrum environments."

7   "Intelligence supporting space operations specifically seeks to define and
     identify all aspects of adversary capabilities, perceptions, intent,

vulnerabilities, disposition, and readiness relative to the space domain, and other domains where actions may affect space operations."

8   "With intelligence, commanders can prioritize activities, effectively allocate resources, assess, and to reduce uncertainty, take necessary risks, and ultimately make better decisions."

9   "Commanders drive intelligence and intelligence drives operations. Commanders shape the intelligence process by articulating clear objectives and mission specific priority intelligence requirements, across every spacepower competency and discipline, tied to commander decision points. Intelligence creates situational understanding supporting the commander's ability to make decisions including course of action selection, prioritization, and allocation of resources, and determining the acceptable levels of risk in all domains."

10   "Orbital warfare uses orbital maneuver and offensive and defensive fires to preserve freedom of access to the domain and allows the United States and its allies and partners to deny the adversary the same advantage. Guardians must analyze foreign threat capabilities, vulnerabilities, adversary intent, and the adversary's respective levels of readiness to inform commander decisions on the employment of forces."

11   "Guardians continually assess the potential effectiveness of a program in a contested environment and against current and future adversary capabilities."

12   "Geospatial intelligence (GEOINT) is the exploitation and analysis of imagery and geospatial information to describe, assess, and visually depict physical features and geographically referenced activities on or about the Earth."

13   "Signals intelligence (SIGINT) includes all communications intelligence (COMINT), electronic intelligence (ELINT), and foreign-instrumentation signals intelligence (FISINT) (Joint Publication 2-0, Joint Intelligence). Guardians support the National Security Agency/Central Security Service (NSA/CSS) and deploy around the world providing actionable SIGINT in support of combatant command requirements. SIGINT data contributes to SDA and can cue collection from other space assets. SIGINT also contributes additional data regarding emerging adversary space capabilities, actions, and intent."

14   "MASINT exploits a variety of phenomena including electro-optical data, radar data, radio frequency data, geophysical data, materials data, and nuclear radiation data, to support signature development and analysis; perform technical analysis; and detect, characterize, locate, and identify targets and events."

15   "Technical intelligence (TECHINT) data originates from the exploitation of foreign materiel and scientific information. TECHINT begins with the acquisition of a foreign piece of equipment or foreign scientific/technological information. US weapons developers, countermeasure designers, tacticians, and operational forces use TECHINT products to prevent technological surprise, neutralize an adversary's technological advantages, enhance force protection, and support the development and employment of effective countermeasures to newly identified adversary equipment."

16   "Counterintelligence includes information gathered and activities conducted to identify, deceive, exploit, disrupt, or protect against espionage, other intelligence activities, sabotage, or assassinations conducted for or on behalf of foreign powers, organizations or persons or their agents, or international terrorist organizations or activities."

17   "The intelligence process provides the basis for common intelligence terminology and procedures. It consists of six interrelated phases of intelligence operations: planning and direction; collection; processing and exploitation; analysis and production; dissemination and integration; and evaluation and feedback. The categories, while displayed as a cyclical function in figure 6, can interact with each other out of cycle. For example, analysis and production will affect planning and direction and define collection requirements for processing and exploitation even though analysis and production is the fourth step in the process. The intelligence process is continuous and iterative, tailorable, and scalable, shaping intelligence activities across all functions to support a commander's decision cycle."

18   "Successfully collecting timely, accurate, and actionable information against an adaptive threat is challenging. Use of multiple sensors and sensor types can increase the likelihood of achieving timely delivery of the information required."

19   "The Intelligence Preparation of the Operational Environment, or IPOE, is a continuous analytic process that is integrated throughout the intelligence process. In accordance with tasked mission requirements and the federation of analysis and production, Guardians develop and maintain IPOE of the space domain to help commanders understand the complex operational environment, the relevant actors, factors, and courses of action to inform decision making. IPOE production is integrated with intelligence from other organizations to provide the joint force commander a holistic understanding of the operational environment (Joint Publication 2-0, Intelligence, and the Joint Guide for Joint Intelligence Preparation of the Operational Environment)."

20   "Collections enable the intelligence processes to generate intelligence products that support warfighter needs. Collections can also communicate changes in the operational environment and understanding of the adversary intent. Throughout planning, execution, and assessment, users should convert intelligence gaps, to include indicators, into collection requirements."

21   "Successfully collecting timely, relevant, and useful information against an adaptive target is challenging. Use of multiple sensors and sensor types can increase the likelihood of timely delivery of the required information."

22   "All Guardians regardless of specific intelligence discipline or mission area, are practitioners of analytic tradecraft. Intelligence Community Directive 203, Analytical Standards, defines analytical tradecraft. Intelligence Community Directive 203 identifies five overarching qualities and principles that guide Guardians conducting intelligence analysis and analytic production:

23 "Advocacy of a particular audience, agenda, or force of preference for a particular policy viewpoint should not distort or shape a Guardian's analytic judgments."

24 "The Deputy Chief of Space Operations for Intelligence (SF/S2) is the Space Force's Senior Intelligence Officer, Head of the Space Force Intelligence Community Element, and Defense Intelligence Component Head and, as such, is responsible to the Secretary of the Air Force and the CSO for delivering intelligence guidance, policies, and programming for the Space Force Intelligence Enterprise."

25 "Delta 5 is force presented to USSPACECOM and provides the majority of Combined Space Operations Center (CSpOC) manning. The CSpOC ISR Division provides timely, predictive, and actionable all source intelligence supporting all aspects of the space tasking cycle and target development in support of world-wide terrestrial operations. Delta 5 ISR Division personnel conduct 24/7 support to space operations through execution of real time electromagnetic interference (EMI) mitigation, indications and warnings for foreign space and missile launches, and collection operations management authority of tasked space sensors. Additionally, the Delta 5 ISR Division works closely with coalition partners to facilitate intelligence sharing and synchronization to achieve combined objectives."

26 "SSC intelligence enables Space Force development, acquisition, equipping, fielding, and sustaining of lethal and resilient space capabilities for warfighters."

27 "Delta 11 delivers realistic, threat-informed test and training environments through the provision of live, virtual, and constructive range and combat replication capability to prepare Guardians, and designated joint and allied partners, to prevail in a contested, degraded, operationally limited, all-domain environment."

28 "The IC's mission is to provide timely, insightful, objective, and relevant intelligence to inform decisions on national security issues and events."

29 "The NRO designs, builds, launches, and operates national reconnaissance spacecraft. It integrates unique and innovative space-based reconnaissance technology and the engineering, development, acquisition, and operation of space reconnaissance systems and related ISR activities. As a consumer of orbital and terrestrial counterspace, and cyber threat intelligence, the NRO is responsible for the integration and coordination of its requirements across the services as well as IC partners to support both its acquisition and operations missions, and as needed to execute its protect and defend mission. Guardians provide support for the NRO's space ISR mission sets."

30 "Strengthening our alliances, military partnerships, and security cooperation makes deterrence more credible and effective. Through these actions, military space forces can reinforce the confidence our allies and partner nations place in their relationship with the United States. As the space domain becomes increasingly congested and contested, developing and maturing key partnerships among our allies and partners becomes a critical enabler of space security."

31   "The DoD and the IC are integrating data, analysis capabilities, and other services from commercial space entities and university programs. Remote sensing, surveillance and reconnaissance, geolocation, targeting, collection and analysis of radio frequency emissions, and electro-optical imagery from commercial space entities are enhancing DoD and space-based intelligence data."

35   "Information advantage. The superior position or condition derived from the ability to access, share, and collaborate securely via trusted information in order develop to more rapidly awareness and to execute decisions than an adversary while exploiting or denying an adversary's ability to do the same."

36   "Measurement and signature intelligence (MASINT). Information produced by quantitative and qualitative analysis of physical attributes of targets and events to characterize, locate, and identify targets and events, and derived from specialized, technically derived measurements of physical phenomena intrinsic to an object or event."

37   "Unfettered access to and freedom to operate in space is a vital national interest; it is the ability to accomplish all four components of national power – diplomatic, information, military, and economic – of a nation's implicit or explicit space strategy."

38   "Orbital warfare. Knowledge of orbital maneuver as well as offensive and defensive fires to preserve freedom of access to the domain. Skill to ensure United States and coalition space forces can continue to provide capability to the joint force while denying that same advantage to the adversary."

Space Doctrine Publication 2-0

INTELLIGENCE

DOCTRINE FOR SPACE FORCES

UNITED STATES
SPACE FORCE

Space Doctrine Publication (SDP) 2-0, *Intelligence*
Space Training and Readiness Command (STARCOM)
OPR: STARCOM Delta 10
19 July 2023

Foreword

Space Doctrine Publication (SDP) 2-0, *Intelligence* establishes doctrine for United States Space Force (USSF) intelligence operations to support the freedom to operate in, from, and to space. This doctrine publication is official advice and commanders should follow it except when, in their judgment, circumstances dictate otherwise. By its nature, doctrine is not directive, and instead provides the Space Force an informed starting point for decision-making and strategy development. Doctrine reflects fundamental principles and best practices based on extant capabilities. It incorporates changes derived from lessons learned during operations, training, wargames, exercises, and, when appropriate, validated concepts.

SDP 2-0, *Intelligence*, aligns with current Space Force doctrine and Chief of Space Operations' Planning Guidance. SDP 2-0 articulates the importance of intelligence in space operations, the contributions space makes to the body of intelligence data available to the joint warfighter, how the Space Force participates in the intelligence process to ensure that data is available, and the role of Guardians in the intelligence community.

Many years of developing space personnel allows our doctrine to speak from a position of authority. I encourage you to study and learn from the time-tested knowledge compiled in this publication. Semper Supra!

SHAWN N. BRATTON
Major General, USAF
Commander, Space Training and Readiness Command

Table of Contents

Table of Figures

Space Force Doctrine

Space Force doctrine guides the proper use of military spacepower in support of the Service's cornerstone responsibilities. It establishes a common framework for employing Guardians as part of a broader joint force. Doctrine provides fundamental principles and authoritative guidance for the employment of military spacepower and an informed starting point for decision-making and strategy development. Since we cannot predict the timing, location, and conditions of the next fight, commanders should be flexible in the implementation of this guidance as circumstances or mission parameters dictate. Where the United States Space Force (USSF) is developing new policies, processes, or structures, call-out boxes (light blue boxes with rounded corners) highlight those for the reader. As the Space Force officially implements these changes, Space Training and Readiness Command (STARCOM) Delta 10 will update this publication.

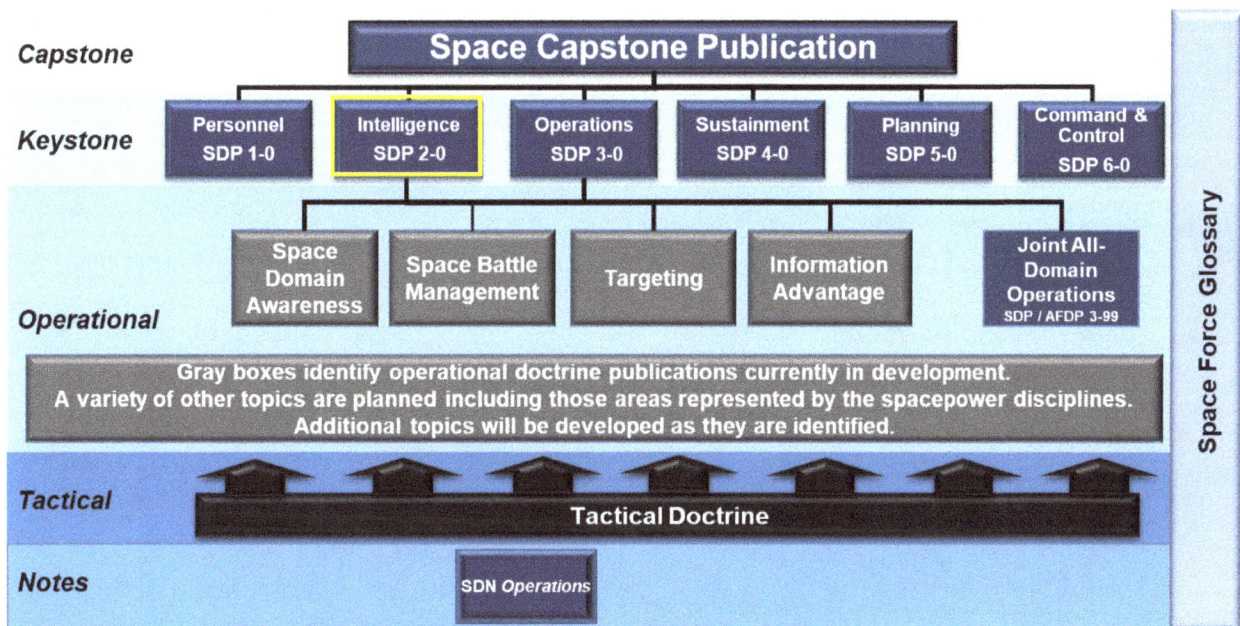

Figure 1. Space Force doctrine hierarchy

Space Doctrine Publication (SDP) 2-0

The Space Force doctrine hierarchy includes four levels of doctrine: capstone, keystone, operational, and tactical, and a glossary. Each level builds on the one above it, reflecting the role of Guardians in every specialty area. The Space Capstone Publication, *Spacepower*, is followed by a set of six keystone doctrine publications. As the capstone doctrine for the Space Force, the Space Capstone Publication, *Spacepower*, defines the necessity of spacepower for our Nation, how military spacepower is employed, who military space forces are, and what the military space forces value. Below the keystone level, the Space Force is developing multiple operational-level doctrine publications, each expanding on a specific area. Tactical doctrine will provide system and tactics, techniques, and procedure (TTP) for a specific area of space operations.

Space Doctrine Publication (SDP) 2-0, one of the six keystone doctrine publications, presents Space Force intelligence operations to support the freedom to operate in, from, and to space.

- Chapter 1 introduces intelligence as part of military spacepower and its contribution to operations across the competition continuum.

- Chapter 2 discusses the role of intelligence and intelligence integration with the other spacepower disciplines.

- Chapter 3 presents all the joint intelligence disciplines and their application to space intelligence.

- Chapter 4 describes the intelligence process, intelligence collection, and collection authorities.

- Chapter 5 presents Space Force organizations supporting intelligence, and how space is engaged across the Intelligence Community (IC), and with other organizations, agencies, allies, and partners to source intelligence data in support of joint and combined operations.

Chapter 1: Introduction

Timely and accurate intelligence is essential in achieving decision advantage for commanders at every echelon. Intelligence is one of the spacepower disciplines in which Guardians specialize, providing data and information essential to operations in the space domain, in areas of responsibility in every other domain, and in the information and electromagnetic spectrum environments. The Space Force organizes, trains, and equips Guardians to conduct operations, including intelligence, surveillance, and reconnaissance (ISR), as part of the joint force to meet national objectives (strategic and military) through the application of military spacepower.

Intelligence. Products resulting from the collection, processing, integration, evaluation, analysis, and interpretation of available information concerning foreign nations, hostile or potentially hostile forces or elements, or areas of actual or potential operations. (Joint Publication 2-0, *Intelligence*)

Intelligence, Surveillance, and Reconnaissance (ISR). An integrated operations and intelligence activity that synchronizes and integrates the planning and operations of sensors, assets, and processing, exploitation, and dissemination systems in direct support of current and future operations. (Joint Publication 2-0, *Intelligence*)

Reconnaissance. A mission undertaken to obtain information about the activities and resources of an enemy or adversary, or to secure data concerning the meteorological, hydrographic, geographic, or other characteristics of a particular area, by visual observation or other detection methods. (Joint Publication 2-0, *Intelligence*)

Surveillance. The systematic observation of aerospace, cyberspace, surface, or subsurface areas, places, persons, or things by visual, aural, electronic, photographic, or other means. (Joint Publication 3-0, *Joint Campaigns and Operations*)

Figure 2. Key definitions

The Space Capstone Publication, *Spacepower,* defines military spacepower as the ability to accomplish strategic and military objectives through the control and exploitation of the space domain. The Space Force frames its ability to deliver military spacepower in terms of its cornerstone responsibilities of preserve freedom of action, enable joint lethality and effectiveness, and provide independent options. Guardians trained and educated in the core competencies and the spacepower disciplines support operations for the joint force whether in competition or conflict. See appendix c for the full descriptions of the cornerstone responsibilities, core competencies, and the spacepower disciplines.

Intelligence and the Competition Continuum

Space operations and intelligence are fundamental to every major military campaign, operation, or activity. Joint Publication 3-0, *Joint Campaigns and Operations*, describes the competition continuum (figure 3) as a world of enduring competition conducted through a mixture of cooperation, competition below armed conflict, and armed conflict or war.

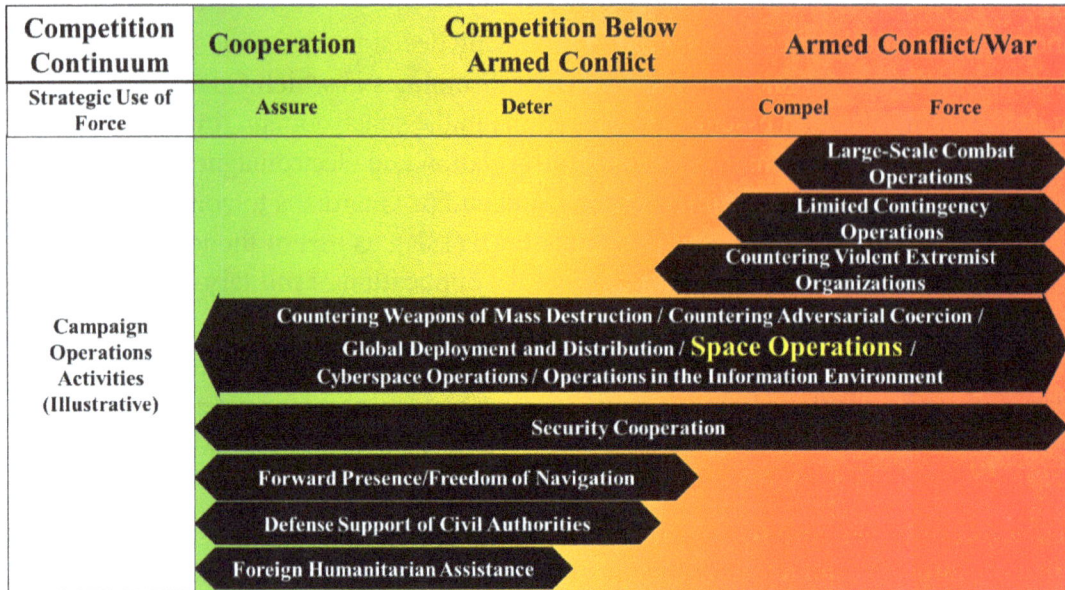

Competition Continuum	Cooperation	Competition Below Armed Conflict		Armed Conflict/War
Strategic Use of Force	Assure	Deter	Compel	Force
Campaign Operations Activities (Illustrative)				Large-Scale Combat Operations
				Limited Contingency Operations
				Countering Violent Extremist Organizations
		Countering Weapons of Mass Destruction / Countering Adversarial Coercion / Global Deployment and Distribution **Space Operations** / Cyberspace Operations / Operations in the Information Environment		
		Security Cooperation		
	Forward Presence/Freedom of Navigation			
	Defense Support of Civil Authorities			
	Foreign Humanitarian Assistance			

Figure 3. Competition continuum

Intelligence supporting space operations specifically seeks to define and identify all aspects of adversary capabilities, perceptions, intent, vulnerabilities, disposition, and readiness relative to the space domain, and other domains where actions may affect space operations. Guardians, presented to the joint force commander, integrate and fuse information received from multiple sources to provide decision advantage, resulting in the understanding of the operational environment in space, other physical domains, and the information and electromagnetic spectrum environments. Figure 4 includes examples of space intelligence operations across the continuum.

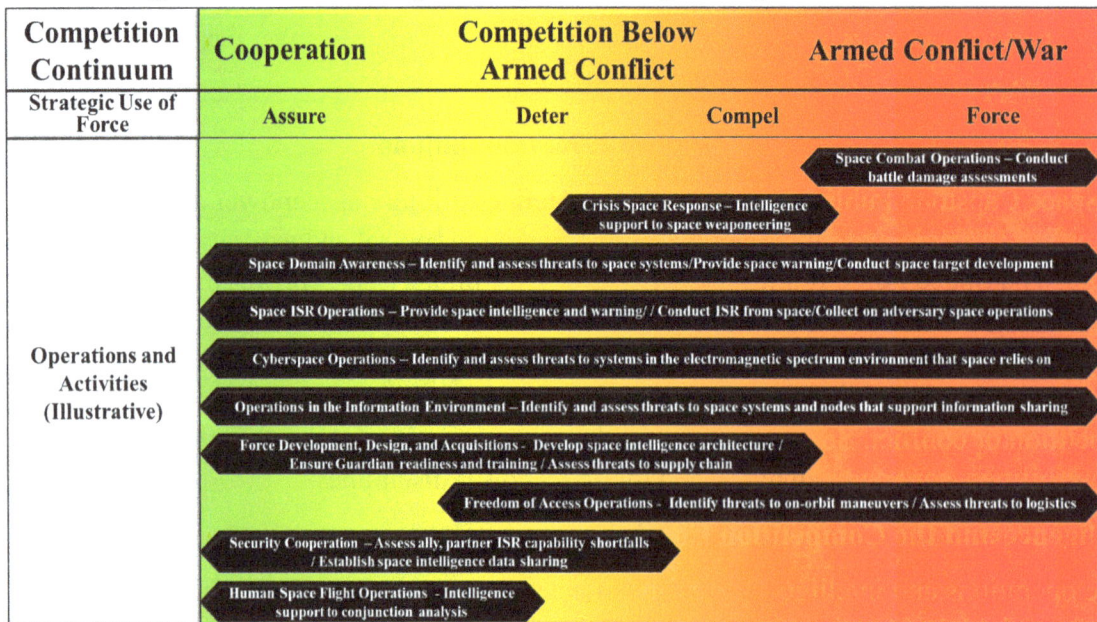

Figure 4. Space ISR operations across the competition continuum

Intelligence in the Space Operations Environment

The operational environment is a composite of conditions, circumstances, and influences that affect the employment of capabilities and bear on the decisions of commanders. These conditions, circumstances, and influences consist of natural and human-made factors. Intelligence helps the commander visualize the operational environment in time and place and understand the factors affecting it. With intelligence, commanders can prioritize activities, effectively allocate resources, assess, and to reduce uncertainty, take necessary risks, and ultimately make better decisions.

The space operational environment is inherently multi-domain, requiring operations in, to, and from the space, air, land, and maritime domains and the information and electromagnetic spectrum environments. See SDP 3-0, *Operations*, for a detailed discussion about the space operational environment.

The Challenge of Continuous Coverage

The integration of fused and processed intelligence from multiple disciplines, sensor types, and domains is vital to maintain a clear sense of the operational environment in the space domain.

Maintaining continuous situational awareness in the space domain is challenging. Tactical events occur in very narrow sectors of the space and terrestrial domains; thus, situational awareness can be short-lived. However, from the tactical to strategic level, long-term and persistent situational awareness of the space domain is critical. The nature of space operations is that the spatial relationships between assets (friendly and adversary) are continuously changing. This creates an operational environment that is extremely dynamic, where achieving and maintaining situational awareness is challenging.

Tracking an entity in space at periodic intervals to maintain situational awareness does not always provide insight into its capabilities, activities, or intent, resulting in a permissive and ambiguous environment in which a quick shift into a threat posture may occur with little warning.

Adversaries may use camouflage, concealment, and deception, creating satellites with secondary or tertiary military purposes concealed behind what may be or appear to be a legitimate civilian or commercial mission. This ambiguity combines with the vastness of space and the momentum of on-orbit platforms to create a situation in which it is impossible to identify and continuously observe all potential threats with the available sensors.

For the future of space intelligence, the Space Force will develop Guardians with knowledge and skills that span the entire spectrum of intelligence disciplines discussed in chapter 3. Exercises and wargames have clearly demonstrated the need for Guardians with expertise in real-time space domain awareness (SDA) and space intelligence to maintain persistent situational awareness. Those same exercises and wargames also highlighted difficulties in the ability to assign attribution, infiltrate threats, and understand motivation in the space environment. Addressing these challenges, and ensuring Guardian readiness to support the joint force, will require specialized training and education for Guardians in the military intelligence discipline.

Figure 5. Continuous coverage vignette

Chapter 2: The Role of Intelligence

Commanders drive intelligence and intelligence drives operations. Commanders shape the intelligence process by articulating clear objectives and mission specific priority intelligence requirements, across every spacepower competency and discipline, tied to commander decision points. Intelligence creates situational understanding supporting the commander's ability to make decisions including course of action selection, prioritization, and allocation of resources, and determining the acceptable levels of risk in all domains. Guardians assigned to the intelligence core specialty are responsible for executing the intelligence process to deliver decision advantage for space operations, and operations in other domains.

Levels of Intelligence

Joint Publication 2-0, *Joint Intelligence*, defines three levels of intelligence: strategic, operational, and tactical. These three levels of intelligence meet the needs of the commanders at each level by informing allocation decisions regarding resources required to collect, analyze, and disseminate intelligence.

a. **Strategic Intelligence.** Strategic intelligence shapes military strategy, policy, plans, and operations at the national and theater levels. Strategic intelligence is generally derived from foundational, broadly scoped, longer-term analysis and can include collaboration efforts with other members of the IC. Primary consumers include combatant commands, the IC, Department of the Air Force, other parts of the Department of Defense (DoD), and national level leadership.

b. **Operational Intelligence.** Operational intelligence informs the planning and conduct of campaigns and major operations to accomplish strategic objectives within the theater and areas of operations. This occurs at multiple echelons such as within a combatant or field command. Guardians ensure intelligence activities, such as analysis, collection, targeting, and integration align with the commander's priority intelligence requirements, decision points, and stated needs in support of mission objectives.

c. **Tactical intelligence.** Tactical intelligence drives the planning and execution of tactical operations. This type of intelligence activity occurs at the unit level and at organizations that maintain tactical control of forces. Guardians provide commanders the intelligence to identify, assess, and defeat threats, and protect assets in support of achieving mission objectives.

Intelligence Integration into the Spacepower Disciplines

The Space Capstone Publication, *Spacepower*, identifies military intelligence among seven disciplines that are necessary components of military spacepower. Intelligence-led, threat-informed operations are critical to the United States, its allies and partners, and their ability to defend the space domain and maintain a competitive advantage in all domains. Intelligence is unique among the spacepower disciplines because it plays a critical role in the successful execution of the six other disciplines and is foundational in meeting service and national objectives.

a. **Orbital Warfare.** Orbital warfare uses orbital maneuver and offensive and defensive fires to preserve freedom of access to the domain and allows the United States and its allies and partners to deny the adversary the same advantage. Guardians must analyze foreign threat capabilities, vulnerabilities, adversary intent, and the adversary's respective levels of readiness to inform commander decisions on the employment of forces.

b. **Space Electromagnetic Warfare.** Guardians should understand the operations within and affected by the electromagnetic spectrum, including how to maneuver within the spectrum, and support targeting to conduct effective non-kinetic fires within the spectrum to deny access to communication pathways. Weaponized directed energy can damage a spacecraft or its payloads. Electromagnetic energy can disrupt or deny electromagnetic spectrum links, isolating a spacecraft from operators and users. These vulnerabilities present a tremendous risk to the viability of space operations. Therefore, Guardians should prepare to exploit and defend the electromagnetic spectrum operations environment through adversary analysis, targeting, aligned collections, and close integration with operational elements.

c. **Space Battle Management.** Space battle management includes knowledge of how to orient friendly capabilities and deny adversary access to the space domain, and skill in making decisions to preserve and ultimately ensure mission accomplishment. It also includes the ability to identify hostile actions and entities, conduct combat identification, target, and direct action in response to an evolving threat environment. Guardian-developed intelligence provides critical inputs to space battle management. Command and control, and proper orientation of space forces in relation to the enemy, requires timely detection of enemy activities and assessment of enemy capabilities and intent. Analysis and collections are pivotal to achieving mission objectives, aiding in the identification of hostile actions, providing combat identification, and informing the commander's battle plan.

d. **Space Access and Sustainment.** Space access and sustainment includes all the processes necessary to field, maintain, and prolong operations in the space domain. To avoid negative effects from enemy actions, space access, mobility, and logistics activities require timely and relevant intelligence. Threat-informed sustainment planning allows for proactive operations that mitigate the effects of enemy actions and maintain friendly force freedom of action. Guardians supporting space access, mobility, and logistics should remain aware of enemy actions that could exploit space logistics vulnerabilities and dependencies in the each of the domains or the information or electromagnetic operations environments. Of particular concern are enemy capabilities and actions that hold critical infrastructure, mobile space assets, reconstitution efforts, or telemetry, tracking, and commanding (TT&C) communications at risk.

e. **Engineering and Acquisition.** The engineering and acquisition discipline ensures the United States has the best capabilities in the world to defend the space domain. Guardians depend on knowledge of adversary capabilities throughout the acquisition process and in the planning and execution of test and evaluation for new capabilities. Guardians continually assess the potential effectiveness of a program in a contested environment and against current and future adversary capabilities.

f. **Cyber Operations**. Guardians employ intelligence-driven cyber operations to defend the global networks that are critical to space operations. Guardians also maintain awareness of cyber threats and operations to derive intelligence relevant to military space operations in all domains and environments.

Chapter 3: Intelligence Disciplines for Space Operations

Intelligence disciplines are well-defined functions that involve specific approaches to collections and analysis with emphasis on technical or human resource capabilities. The Space Force leverages data from all available and appropriate intelligence disciplines over the course of any operation to:

a. Define the operational environment

b. Enhance space domain awareness (SDA), which is fundamental to the conduct of all space operations

c. Plan and execute TTP in support of the joint force

d. Support selecting and prioritizing targets to satisfy operational objectives through understanding adversary capabilities, disposition, personnel, units, facilities, systems, infrastructure, nodes, and links

e. Enable battle damage assessment, combat assessment, and restrike recommendations

f. Shape the space-based weapon systems and sensors of the future and TTP for employment

g. Support operations in all domains through ISR from space

Data from across the spectrum of intelligence disciplines and collections on a wide range of phenomena (observables), and modalities (behaviors) contribute to space missions and help define the operational environment for space operations.

Geospatial Intelligence

Geospatial intelligence (GEOINT) is the exploitation and analysis of imagery and geospatial information to describe, assess, and visually depict physical features and geographically referenced activities on or about the Earth. GEOINT consists of imagery, imagery intelligence (IMINT), and geospatial information (Joint Publication 2-0, *Joint Intelligence*).

a. **Imagery**. Imagery is a likeness or presentation of any natural or human-made feature, related object, or activity and the positional data acquired at the same time as the likeness or representation. This includes products produced by service and national intelligence reconnaissance spacecraft, and likenesses or presentations produced by commercial or civil systems. Assets operated by the Space Force and other members of the IC collect imagery on space-based and terrestrial objects. The Space Force leverages imagery data in assessing adversary space and terrestrial activities. These may indicate impending, unexpected, or threatening activity by an adversary such as maneuver of a space-based asset, a space launch, or other activity that could affect operations or assets. Space-based imagery is a significant contributor to intelligence development for terrestrial campaigns and operations planned by the joint and combined force.

b. **IMINT.** IMINT is the technical, geographic, and intelligence information derived through the interpretation or analysis of imagery and other materials. IMINT includes exploitation of imagery data derived from electro-optical, radar, infrared, multi-spectral, and laser sensors. Analysts assess data from across the electromagnetic spectrum to provide information about impacts to United States (US), allied and partner space assets, and inform commanders about adversary space systems, capabilities, and actions.

   c. **Geospatial Information.** Geospatial information identifies the geographic location and characteristics of natural or constructed features and boundaries on the Earth, including statistical data, and information derived from methods such as remote sensing, mapping, and surveying technologies, and mapping, charting, geodetic data, and related products. Positioning, navigation, and timing data, provided by the Space Force, is critical to geospatial analysis supporting military planning, training, rehearsal, modeling and simulation, and targeting. Without positioning, navigation, and timing support, geospatial information would not deliver the necessary intelligence value.

Signals Intelligence

Signals intelligence (SIGINT) includes all communications intelligence (COMINT), electronic intelligence (ELINT), and foreign-instrumentation signals intelligence (FISINT) (Joint Publication 2-0, *Joint Intelligence*). Guardians support the National Security Agency/Central Security Service (NSA/CSS) and deploy around the world providing actionable SIGINT in support of combatant command requirements. SIGINT data contributes to SDA and can cue collection from other space assets. SIGINT also contributes additional data regarding emerging adversary space capabilities, actions, and intent.

   a. **COMINT.** COMINT is intelligence and technical information derived from collecting and processing intercepted foreign communications passed by radio, wire, or other electromagnetic means.

   b. **ELINT.** ELINT is technical and geolocation intelligence derived from foreign non-communications electromagnetic radiation emanating from other than nuclear detonations or radioactive sources. ELINT includes operational electronic intelligence (OPELINT), and technical electronic intelligence (TECHELINT). OPELINT is concerned with operationally relevant information such as the location, movement, employment, tactics, and activity of foreign non-communications emitters and their associated weapon systems. TECHELINT is concerned with the technical aspects of foreign non-communications emitters such as signal characteristics, modes, functions, associations, capabilities, limitations, vulnerabilities, and technology levels.

   c. **FISINT.** FISINT is technical information and intelligence derived from the intercept of foreign electromagnetic emissions associated with the testing and operational deployment of aerospace, surface, and subsurface systems.

Measurement and Signature Intelligence

Measurement and signature intelligence (MASINT) is information produced by quantitative and qualitative analysis of physical attributes about an object or event. Derived from specialized, technically derived measurements of physical phenomena, it helps characterize, locate, and identify that object or event. MASINT exploits a variety of phenomena including electro-optical data, radar data, radio frequency data, geophysical data, materials data, and nuclear radiation data, to support signature development and analysis; perform technical analysis; and detect, characterize, locate, and identify targets and events (Joint Publication 2-0, *Joint Intelligence*).

a. **Electro-Optical Data.** Electro-optical data includes emitted or reflected energy across the visible or infrared portion of the electromagnetic spectrum. This includes ultraviolet, visible, near infrared, and infrared parts of the spectrum.

b. **Radar Data.** Radar data captures reflected radar energy (reradiated) from a target.

c. **Radio Frequency Data.** Radio frequency data includes electromagnetic pulse emissions associated with nuclear testing, or other high-energy events for the purpose of determining power levels, operating characteristics, and signatures of advanced technology weapons, power, and propulsion systems.

d. **Geophysical Data.** Geophysical data captures phenomena transmitted through the Earth (ground, water, and atmosphere) and human-made structures including emitted or reflected sounds, pressure waves, vibrations, and magnetic field or ionosphere disturbances. Subcategories include seismic intelligence, acoustic intelligence, and magnetic intelligence.

e. **Materials Data.** Materials data includes data from gas, liquid, or solid samples, collected by automatic equipment, such as air samplers, or directly by humans.

f. **Nuclear Radiation Data.** Data related to nuclear radiation and physical phenomena associated with nuclear weapons, processes, materials, devices, or facilities.

Many of the data types collected by Space Force assets fall under the MASINT discipline. This data also contributes to warning intelligence such as providing tactical warning and attack assessment information to operational command centers regarding nuclear detonations or missile launches. Space Force assets also collect space object identification data across the electromagnetic spectrum including electro-optical, radar and long wave infrared. This data provides critical information about the size (radar cross section), configuration, and health of adversary assets on orbit. This also supports battle damage assessment, allowing Guardians to assess the functionality of an asset following an event (e.g., spacecraft break up, anti-satellite test). Terrestrial space assets including the ground-based radars and telescopes operated by Guardians collect radar and electro-optical data to maintain the space catalog. MASINT data forms the foundation for maintaining SDA on orbit, enabling the analysis necessary to maintain space security including:

a. **Maneuver Detection.** Analysis of observation data indicates an object on orbit has changed planes, moved into a transfer orbit, or made some other expected or unexpected change to its behavior and location. This information is critical for maintaining custody of all assets and identifying changes in behavior patterns.

b. **Conjunction Assessment.** Analysis of observation data for asset behavior and orbit indicates the potential of collision or a close approach. This information is essential for protection of high-value assets and recognizing indications of an evolving threat.

c. **Uncorrelated Object Analysis**. When observation data indicates an object not previously correlated to known objects in the satellite catalog (a registry of all known or identified orbital space objects), the object is tagged as uncorrelated. This information may indicate a maneuver, break-up, debris-generating event, or separation. This information is critical for identifying a debris threat or the potential of a previously unknown adversary asset on orbit.

d. **Natural Hazards Identification.** Space debris, space weather, and naturally occurring objects and electromagnetic interference pose threats to United States and partner capabilities. Awareness of these threats allows for mitigation actions or informs assessments about the possible source of issues with an asset.

Open-Source Intelligence

Open-source intelligence (OSINT) derives from publicly available information that any member of the public can lawfully obtain by request, purchase, or observation. Examples of open sources include unofficial and draft documents, published and unpublished reference material, research, or cloud databases, and web-based networking platforms or repositories. OSINT complements the other intelligence disciplines and can fill gaps and provide accuracy and fidelity in classified information databases. However, OSINT is susceptible to manipulation and deception, and thus requires analysis and review during processing. The OSINT functional manager for the IC is the Director of the Central Intelligence Agency (CIA). The DoD lead for OSINT is the Director of the Defense Intelligence Agency (DIA) (Joint Publication 2-0, *Joint Intelligence*). Guardians leverage OSINT data regarding adversary actions that could affect space operations and in particular, data about space assets and impending launches.

Technical Intelligence

Technical intelligence (TECHINT) data originates from the exploitation of foreign materiel and scientific information. TECHINT begins with the acquisition of a foreign piece of equipment or foreign scientific/technological information. US weapons developers, countermeasure designers, tacticians, and operational forces use TECHINT products to prevent technological surprise, neutralize an adversary's technological advantages, enhance force protection, and support the development and employment of effective countermeasures to newly identified adversary equipment. The Joint Captured Materiel Exploitation Center, managed by the DIA Joint Foreign Materiel Program Office, is the primary DoD contingency TECHINT organization (Joint Publication 2-0, *Joint Intelligence*). Space intelligence and acquisition organizations use TECHINT data regarding new space capabilities to develop intelligence regarding adversary equipment that could affect space operations.

Human Intelligence

Human intelligence (HUMINT) is a category of intelligence derived from information collected and provided by human sources. HUMINT includes intelligence interrogation, source operations, and debriefing (Joint Publication 2-0, *Joint Intelligence)*. When available, the Space Force can leverage HUMINT data regarding adversary actions that could threaten space capabilities or operations. These include impending launches, new space capabilities, and threats to terrestrial facilities, personnel, or cyberspace assets. The Space Force does not have any organic HUMINT capabilities and relies on collection from other military services and IC partners.

Counterintelligence

Counterintelligence includes information gathered and activities conducted to identify, deceive, exploit, disrupt, or protect against espionage, other intelligence activities, sabotage, or assassinations conducted for or on behalf of foreign powers, organizations or persons or their agents, or international terrorist organizations or activities. (Joint Publication 2-0, *Joint Intelligence*). Counterintelligence support to acquisition and engineering is critical to the protection of space systems and their components anywhere along the supply chain that could allow an adversary to exploit a device, or one of its components. Compromise of the supply chain can occur before or after the delivery of a product or service, or during software updates or hardware replacement. The Air Force Office of Special Investigation conducts counterintelligence for the Department of the Air Force, including the Space Force.

Chapter 4: Intelligence Process, Collections, and Authorities

The Chief of Space Operations (CSO) in the *Chief of Space Operations' Planning Guidance*, published in 2020, directed "...use of joint planning methodology throughout the Space Force. This ensures a common standard and prepares Space Force members for integration with joint forces." Based on that direction the Space Force employs the intelligence process as outlined in Joint Publication 2-0, *Joint Intelligence*.

The Intelligence Process

The intelligence process provides the basis for common intelligence terminology and procedures. It consists of six interrelated phases of intelligence operations: planning and direction; collection; processing and exploitation; analysis and production; dissemination and integration; and evaluation and feedback. The categories, while displayed as a cyclical function in figure 6, can interact with each other out of cycle. For example, analysis and production will affect planning and direction and define collection requirements for processing and exploitation even though analysis and production is the fourth step in the process. The intelligence process is continuous and iterative, tailorable, and scalable, shaping intelligence activities across all functions to support a commander's decision cycle.

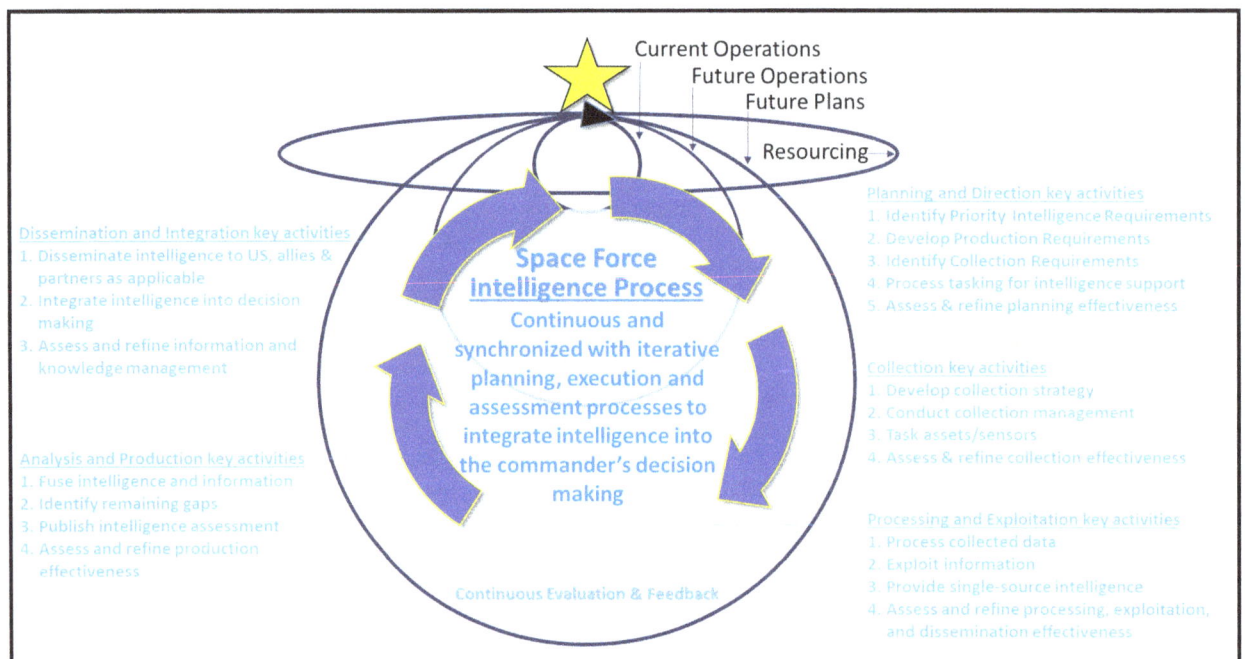

Figure 6. Intelligence process overlaid on decision cycles

a. **Planning and Direction.** Planning and directing of intelligence activities occurs continuously through the intelligence process, often in support of several simultaneous decision cycles. Synchronization and deconfliction across intelligence efforts is key for optimizing use of limited intelligence resources. Intelligence planning efforts begin with initial understanding of intelligence preparation of the operational environment (IPOE), friendly intelligence capabilities, commander's objectives, and associated intelligence gaps and shortfalls. Priority intelligence requirements evolve with the planning and execution of operations and assessments. Guardians, as intelligence planners, identify analysis and collection requirements in accordance with the commander's needs and synchronize collection plans and production schedules to the needs of planning and operations. Commanders and intelligence leaders provide direction to synchronize intelligence efforts with other military functions and with applicable partners. Orders and other tasking programs of record are key for the orderly maintenance and distribution of intelligence requirements and directives.

b. **Collection.** Collection involves the acquisition of required information and provision of that information for processing. Collection managers task the most appropriate available asset, or combination of assets, to satisfy the information requirements. Successfully collecting timely, accurate, and actionable information against an adaptive threat is challenging. Use of multiple sensors and sensor types can increase the likelihood of achieving timely delivery of the information required.

c. **Processing and Exploitation.** Processing and exploitation sort, correlate, and transform raw data into forms suitable for exploitation by decision-makers and other consumers. This step in the process can include translations, decryption, and interpretation. It may be necessary to coordinate with other organizations to ensure data is in a state and form that end users can exploit and analyze.

d. **Analysis and Production.** Analysis and production involve the fusion of data and information from various, reliable sources for the purpose of correlating, linking, and assessing available intelligence with an emphasis on the overall intelligence requirement. Supported by the IPOE process (detailed below), the analysis and production phase provides end users with timely and actionable intelligence for intelligence and mission planning.

e. **Dissemination and Integration.** Processed intelligence needs to reach consumers in a timely manner. The needs of the user combined with the criticality and sensitivity of the intelligence determine the best means of dissemination. The Unified Data Library contributes to the timely dissemination of Space Force data, making intelligence data and products discoverable and accessible to users. Intelligence products integrated with other data or intelligence generated by other collectors prior to dissemination or at the receiving end can further develop understanding of the operational environment. The need to process, disseminate, and integrate intelligence into ever-reducing decision timelines requires Guardians to maintain running intelligence estimates, especially for priority problem sets and mission areas.

f. **Evaluation and Feedback.** Evaluation and feedback occur continuously throughout the intelligence process. A collaborative dialogue between intelligence planners, analysts, collection managers, collectors, and intelligence systems architects identify deficiencies and shares best practices throughout the intelligence process. Engagement with intelligence consumers is essential to assess how well products and dissemination methods meet the commander's requirements. These inputs inform intelligence prioritization and resourcing decisions, and Guardians integrate them back into planning for space intelligence operations.

Intelligence Preparation of the Operational Environment

The Intelligence Preparation of the Operational Environment, or IPOE, is a continuous analytic process that is integrated throughout the intelligence process. In accordance with tasked mission requirements and the federation of analysis and production, Guardians develop and maintain IPOE of the space domain to help commanders understand the complex operational environment, the relevant actors, factors, and courses of action to inform decision making. IPOE production is integrated with intelligence from other organizations to provide the joint force commander a holistic understanding of the operational environment (Joint Publication 2-0, *Intelligence,* and the Joint Guide for Joint Intelligence Preparation of the Operational Environment).

    a. **Define the Operational Environment.** Accurately defining the operational environment is critical to scoping IPOE efforts and successfully informing mission planning. In this initial step, identify significant characteristics of the operational area relevant to the mission. Clearly defining the complexities of the operational environment becomes more important as operations expand across multiple domains, affect multiple factors, and generate near-to-long-term effects. Defining the operational environment is a significant challenge for space operations due to the complexity of the organizational relationships and large scale of responsibility, requiring an understanding of activities in all domains to preserve freedom of action within the space domain. All-source intelligence and collaboration is needed to frame, understand, and maintain the IPOE production for space.

    b. **Describe Operational Environment Impact.** This step assesses the impact the operational environment may have on adversary, friendly, and neutral military capabilities. The operational environment benefits or hinders the United States, its allies, partners, and adversaries in a similar manner. Differences in military capabilities and the use of intelligence from multiple sources and disciplines can help the United States, its allies, and partners employ the operational environment to their advantage.

    c. **Evaluate the Adversary and Other Relevant Actors.** Guardians comprehensively evaluate adversaries and relevant third parties by analyzing their capabilities, limitations, the current situation, centers of gravity, and their tactics, techniques, and procedures. Employing intelligence from multiple disciplines can increase the joint force's ability to understand opposing and neutral forces as part of the operational environment, and in turn, increase the likelihood of mission success.

    d. **Assess Adversary and Actor Courses of Action**. Guardians estimate the adversary's most likely and most dangerous course of action and develop a detailed understanding of the adversary's and other relevant actors' probable intent and future strategy. In addition, the assessment informs commanders about the potential reaction of others (allies, partners, or other adversaries) to action on the part of the United States, the adversary, or other relevant actor under assessment.

Intelligence Collection

Collection is the acquisition of information and the provision of this information to processing elements. Collections enable the intelligence processes to generate intelligence products that support warfighter needs. Collections can also communicate changes in the operational environment and understanding of the adversary intent. Throughout planning, execution, and assessment, users should convert intelligence gaps, to include indicators, into collection requirements. Analysts and other users of intelligence products should evaluate and provide feedback on these products to help ensure collections are beneficial to the overall mission and are an appropriate allocation of resources.

According to planning directives and commander's guidance, Guardians conduct collection operations required to satisfy intelligence requirements. Understanding the collection authorities and processes is essential to ensure satisfaction of the commander's intent and objectives against approved priority intelligence requirements. It is also essential for effective allocation of limited assets or resources against the most critical requirements.

a. **Request for Information (RFI).** The identification of intelligence and information shortfalls triggers the RFI. The RFI articulates requirements that ensure intelligence needs are resolved. If existing intelligence products cannot satisfy a requirement, a production requirement leads to production of new products. If no existing production or data can fulfill the intelligence requirement, collection managers at every echelon develop collection requirements to task and drive collection operations to gather the data.

b. **Collection Management.** Collection management is the process of converting requests for information into collection requirements; establishing priorities; tasking or coordinating with appropriate collection sources or agencies; monitoring results; and retasking as required. Collection managers task the most appropriate available asset, or combination of assets, to satisfy the information requirements or request collection from resources not under their authority. The delegated collection management authority is responsible for assessing the best mix of sensors and sensor types to increase achieve timely delivery of the information required. DoD, joint, and service collection operations all fall under a delegated collection management authority. The collection process, aligned to the applicable collection management authority, is composed of two functions: collection requirements management and collection operations management. The collection management authority may delegate either or both responsibilities for execution to subordinate echelons. The Space Force's Senior Intelligence Officer exercises collection management authority in support of the service's overarching collection management plan for space missions. A combatant command's intelligence directorate exercises collection management authority in support of the overarching collection management plan for space missions for the joint force.

1) **Collection Requirements Management.** Collection requirements management exists at each command level of every echelon in an organization. The collection requirements manager captures the needs of organizations and converts intelligence-related information requirements into collection requirements,

establishing priorities, tasking, or coordinating with appropriate collection sources or agencies, monitoring results, and retasking, as required. The collection requirements manager, acting on behalf of the collection management authority, prioritizes and registers collection requirements based on the commander's intent, objectives, approved priority intelligence requirements, and the current situation to ensure allocation of assets or resources against the most critical requirements.

2) **Collections Operations Management.** Collections operations management is the authoritative direction, scheduling, and control of specific collection operations and associated processing, exploitation, and reporting resources. Space Force assigned ISR organizations execute collections operations management for assets that they control, or resources delegated by the collection management authority. The collection operations manager schedules and controls collection operations, which includes the processing, exploitation, and dissemination of the collected data. The collection operations manager will select the assets best suited to collect the information needed to satisfy service-specific information requirements. This includes synchronizing the timing of collection with the operational scheme of maneuver and with other intelligence operations such as processing and exploitation, analysis and production, and dissemination. The combatant command's intelligence directorate guides collection operations management execution with a unified joint collection plan and approves assigned and attached component requirements.

Collection managers need to know the capabilities, limitations, survivability, and lead times of available collection systems, and the processing, exploitation, analysis, and production timelines to complete and disseminate a product. Collection managers are responsible for coordinating the employment of all available collection capabilities. This includes requesting external theater and national level resources to acquire needed information.

c. **Collection Plan.** The collection plan prioritizes and focuses collection efforts. Clearly articulated requirements help ensure the collection plan identifies and tasks the best resources for fulfilling the information requirement. Successfully collecting timely, relevant, and useful information against an adaptive target is challenging. Use of multiple sensors and sensor types can increase the likelihood of timely delivery of the required information. Guardians should be aware of any limitations that affect the collection plan when planning for space operations, responding to intelligence requirements, and working to correlate assets for collection operations. Some key areas for Guardians to consider in evaluating a collection plan include:

1) Revisit rates, dwell times, and sun angle over a potential target

2) Space and terrestrial weather

3) Terrain masking, concealment, and camouflage

4) Physical distance between on-orbit sensors and the limited number and location of downlink networks and antennas

5) All available sensor types and their ability to satisfy a priority intelligence requirement

6) High demand for space-based sensor data and limited sensor availability

7) Predictability of overflight impacting ability to collect desired data

d. **Intelligence Assets and Resources.** Collection of timely, accurate, and relevant intelligence is highly dependent the availability and capabilities of organic, attached, supporting or otherwise allocated collection assets. Use of service and national assets, as defined in US Code Title 10 (legal basis for the roles, missions, and organization of each of the services as well as the DoD) and Title 50 (authorities for IC operations in support of the National Defense Strategy), during collections is often essential to satisfy intelligence requirements. The Space Force can also leverage ally and partner space capabilities, in addition to sensors not traditionally employed for ISR or space missions, to satisfy the commander's collection plan.

Targeting

Targeting is the process of selecting and prioritizing entities or objects and matching the appropriate response to them, considering operational requirements and capabilities. Information and intelligence gathered during battlespace characterization and find, fix, track activities support deliberate (preplanned) and dynamic (target of opportunity) targeting. The targeting cycle spans the development of commander's objectives, guidance, and intent; target development, vetting, validation, nomination, and prioritization; commander decision and force assignment, planning and execution; and finally combat assessment. The Space Force conducts space-related targeting efforts through federated targeting support, target system analysis using all-source intelligence analysis, federated target system analysis production, and service organize, train, and equip actions to build and sustain a space targeting enterprise to support combatant commanders.

Intelligence Analysis

All Guardians regardless of specific intelligence discipline or mission area, are practitioners of analytic tradecraft. Intelligence Community Directive 203, *Analytical Standards*, defines analytical tradecraft. Intelligence Community Directive 203 identifies five overarching qualities and principles that guide Guardians conducting intelligence analysis and analytic production:

a. **Objective**. Analysts perform their functions with objectivity and with awareness of their own assumptions and reasoning. They employ reasoning techniques and practical mechanisms that reveal and mitigate bias. Guardians should be aware of influence by existing analytic positions or judgments and consider alternative perspectives and contrary information. Previous judgments should not constrain analysis when new developments indicate a modification is necessary.

b. **Independent of political consideration.** Advocacy of a particular audience, agenda, or force of preference for a particular policy viewpoint should not distort or shape a Guardian's analytic judgments.

c. **Timely.** Guardians should disseminate analysis in time for it to be actionable by customers. The Space Force's analytic elements are responsible for being continually aware of events of intelligence interest, of customer activities and schedules, and of intelligence requirements and priorities, to provide useful analysis at the right time.

d. **Based on all available sources of intelligence information.** Guardians should use all available relevant information to inform their analysis. The Space Force's analytic elements should identify and address critical information gaps and work with collection activities and data providers to develop access and collection strategies.

e. **Implements and exhibits analytic tradecraft standards.** Intelligence analysis should describe the quality and credibility of underlying sources, data, and methodologies upon which judgments are based. Using Intelligence Community Directive 203 defined terminology, Guardians also characterize any uncertainties associated with major analytic judgments and explain the basis for the uncertainties, the likelihood of occurrence of an event or development, and the analyst's confidence in the basis for this judgment.

Intelligence Mission Data Production

Intelligence mission data production is the ability to derive, produce, and rapidly update the intelligence used for programming Space Force mission systems in development, testing, operations, and sustainment. This includes but is not limited to the following functional areas: signatures, electronic warfare, order of battle, characteristics, and performance. The increasing capability of space systems, and platform and control systems that require intelligence information to operate as designed, has significantly increased the need for the production and rapid integration of intelligence mission data into space operations.

Intelligence Support to Acquisition

Intelligence support to acquisition and its associated analytical processes guide the acquisition community by informing space and ISR system design through technical characterization, analysis of future threat projections, and determination of the intelligence sensitivity of programs in development. Intelligence support also allows the Space Force to conduct threat-informed acquisition and testing activities. This includes production of detailed threat reports and digital threat models required to support the acquisition of systems from conception, through developmental and operational testing.

Intelligence sensitivity analysis performed for systems in development helps determine if they require intelligence mission data during development or in performing the system's intended mission. Additionally, an intelligence sensitivity analysis determines if a system will require direct support of intelligence personnel or will influence intelligence data at any point in the planning and direction; collection; processing and exploitation; analysis and production; and dissemination cycle. Subsequently, an intelligence supportability analysis will be developed for intelligence systems deemed sensitive.

Chapter 5: Intelligence Organizations, Roles, and Relationships

Space Force organizations at every level participate in the development of intelligence products for both internal use and dissemination to external users. Space Force intelligence organizations use foundational intelligence data from all disciplines to define the space domain operational environment, develop SDA, and provide the community warning about adversary assets and actions.

Figure 7 depicts the current structure of the Space Force. The Space Staff, three field commands (FLDCOMs) (Space Operations Command [SpOC], Space Systems Command [SSC], Space Training and Readiness Command [STARCOM)]), and two direct reporting units (Space Development Agency [SDA)] and Space Rapid Capabilities Office [SpRCO]) support the Office of the Chief of Space Operations (OCSO). The Space Warfighting Analysis Center (SWAC) is a primary subordinate unit to SpOC with direct liaison authority with the CSO and the Space Staff.

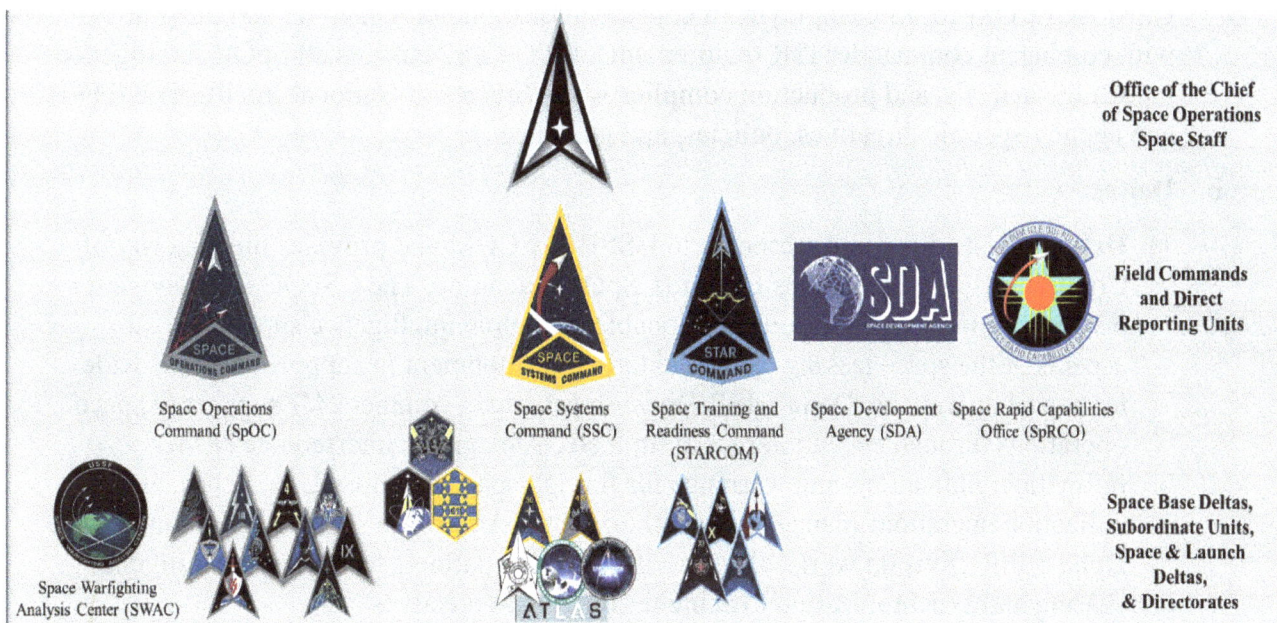

Figure 7. Space Force structure

Deputy Chief of Space Operations for Intelligence

The Deputy Chief of Space Operations for Intelligence (SF/S2) is the Space Force's Senior Intelligence Officer, Head of the Space Force Intelligence Community Element, and Defense Intelligence Component Head and, as such, is responsible to the Secretary of the Air Force and the CSO for delivering intelligence guidance, policies, and programming for the Space Force Intelligence Enterprise. These duties include serving as the focal point for foreign, adversary space, and counterspace capabilities analysis, assisting the FLDCOMs in providing operationally ready ISR forces in response to the needs of the combatant commanders and combat support agencies, and ensuring those forces can provide necessary intelligence support for space missions. SF/S2 serves as Chief, USSF Service Cryptologic Component and is the principal Space Force authority for all cryptologic matters. In this role, SF/S2 serves as the principal advisor to the Director, National Security Agency/Chief, Central Security Service (DIRNSA/CHCSS) for matters related to Space Force cryptologic activities and retains management oversight of those activities. SF/S2 is subordinate to DIRNSA/CHCSS for matters related to Space Force cryptologic activities in accordance with DoD Directive (DoDD) 5100.20, *National Security Agency/Central Security Service (NSA/CSS)*, and US SIGINT directives. SF/S2 also oversees the intelligence activities of the National Space Intelligence Center.

Space Operations Command

SpOC generates, presents, and sustains combat ready Guardians for space operations, intelligence, cyberspace, and combat support missions.

a. **Deputy Commanding General for Operations (DCG-O)/S2**. DCG-O/S2 is responsible to Commander, Space Operations Command (SpOC/CC) and DCG-O to improve all ISR capabilities within the Deltas and at the Space Force component level. DCG-O/S2 is also responsible to SpOC/CC as Commander, Space Force Forces (COMSPACEFOR) for USSPACECOM for ISR employment considerations, planning factors, and integration with combatant commander ISR requirements. DCG-O/S2 ensures all SpOC intelligence reporting, analysis, and production complies with Director of National Intelligence (DNI) and agency-specific directives, policies, and guidance.

b. **Deltas.**

1) **Delta 5.** Delta 5 is force presented to USSPACECOM and provides the majority of Combined Space Operations Center (CSpOC) manning. The CSpOC ISR Division provides timely, predictive, and actionable all source intelligence supporting all aspects of the space tasking cycle and target development in support of world-wide terrestrial operations. Delta 5 ISR Division personnel conduct 24/7 support to space operations through execution of real time electromagnetic interference (EMI) mitigation, indications and warnings for foreign space and missile launches, and collection operations management authority of tasked space sensors. Additionally, the Delta 5 ISR Division works closely with coalition partners to facilitate intelligence sharing and synchronization to achieve combined objectives.

2) **Delta 7.** Delta 7 is the Space Force operational ISR element, employing a variety of fixed and mobile sensors across the globe to provide time sensitive, critical, and actionable intelligence for space domain operations. ISR squadrons under Delta 7 provide tailored intelligence products and mission planning support to other FLDCOMs, Deltas, combatant commanders, and IC partners. Delta 7 provides Guardians as liaisons to the National Reconnaissance Office (NRO), the National Security Agency/Central Security Service (NSA/CSS), and the National Geospatial Intelligence Agency (NGA). These Guardians execute service-retained operations in support of combatant commander requirements and weapons system acquisition and testing.

3) **Delta 15.** Delta 15 provides the joint force commander, COMSPACEFOR, SpOC, and Delta 15 staff with IPOE, predictive battlespace awareness, target development,

tactical assessment, and ISR operations that help drive the space tasking cycle. Delta 15 monitors of the operational environment and maintains a common threat, targeting, and ISR picture supporting all-domain operations. Delta 15 Guardians conduct IPOE, integrated analysis and production, ISR planning, and targeting to shape decision-making and enable operations.

4) **Delta 18.** Delta 18, the National Space Intelligence Center (NSIC), provides foundational, scientific, and technical intelligence to inform senior policy makers, service and national acquisitions, and military operations. NSIC shares this responsibility with other service intelligence centers and DIA as federated in the Defense Intelligence Analytic Program.

c. **SWAC.** The SWAC intelligence advisor supports threat assessments contributing the force design work across the Centers of Excellence for Multi-Domain Awareness and Spectrum Warfare, and the Space Security and Defense Program (SSDP).

Space Systems Command

SSC is responsible for delivering new space capabilities at operationally relevant speeds, to include developing, acquiring, equipping, fielding, and sustaining those capabilities. The SSC Space Systems Integration Office provides intelligence support for all current and future programs, and for space launch operations through Space Launch Deltas 30 and 45.

The SSC Intelligence Directorate/S2 provides timely, relevant, and tailored acquisition intelligence and special security support to SSC and the entire Space Force acquisition enterprise (including SDA and SpRCO), in addition to other Space Force acquisition elements, industry and academic partners. SSC intelligence enables Space Force development, acquisition, equipping, fielding, and sustaining of lethal and resilient space capabilities for warfighters.

SSC's Intelligence Directorate partners with SSC program offices to ensure capability development is threat informed in accordance with regulatory prescription in the DoD acquisition system, and dynamically based on threat activity. This support leverages all forms of intelligence, from open source through exquisite intelligence, and when available counterintelligence. SSC program offices rely on regular access to current threat intelligence to develop and test space systems that are suitable for the operational environment, can mitigate risk, and exploit opportunities.

Space Training and Readiness Command

The mission of STARCOM is to increase Space Force readiness to prevail in competition and conflict through education, training, doctrine, and test. STARCOM intelligence personnel are embedded in the headquarters and across the five Deltas. Unit-level intelligence personnel reside in squadron intelligence flights or sections to provide support to all assigned missions. Intelligence management and oversight is through a Delta-level Senior Intelligence Officer who is responsible to plan, program, validate and manage all intelligence requirements for their organization and any subordinate or supported units.

a. **STARCOM Director of Intelligence Operations.** The STARCOM Director of Intelligence Operations is the FLDCOM Senior Intelligence Officer and is responsible for intelligence support to the STARCOM commander, sensitive compartmented information management, and plans and programs for intelligence across the FLDCOM. The STARCOM Director of Intelligence Operations is also responsible for managing intelligence resources and ensuring training and personnel are available to subordinate organizations for ISR operations.

b. **Deltas.**

   1) **Delta 11.** Delta 11 delivers realistic, threat-informed test and training environments through the provision of live, virtual, and constructive range and combat replication capability to prepare Guardians, and designated joint and allied partners, to prevail in a contested, degraded, operationally limited, all-domain environment. Delta 11 intelligence personnel prepare Guardians and joint forces by developing, maintaining, and operating capabilities to replicate enemy threats to space-based and space-enabled systems. Delta 11 intelligence personnel also function as aggressors and support range operations including live, digital, and hardware in the loop-based threat elements capable of enterprise-level, system-of-systems test, and training. Finally, Delta 11 intelligence personnel partner with intelligence agencies and SpOC intelligence units to ensure current and near-term threats are replicated in live and virtual environments before threats reach full operational capability.

   2) **Delta 12.** Delta 12 conducts independent test and evaluation of Space Force capabilities and delivery of timely, accurate, and expert information in support of weapon system acquisition, operational acceptance, and readiness decisions. Delta 12 intelligence personnel provide critical threat-based information to allow organizations to plan, execute, and report on prototyping, experimentation, and test and evaluation of space systems, from development through fielding and space system sustainment. Threat-based testing is critical to drive improvements in space program development, awareness of operational considerations, and informed acquisition and fielding decisions. Delta 12 intelligence personnel are an essential part of the acquisition and test communities.

Partnerships

Space security, as a core competency, establishes and promotes stable conditions for the safe and secure access to space activities for DoD, civil, commercial, IC, and multinational partners. Establishing partnerships with other members of the IC, joint partners, inter-agency organizations, allies, commercial partners, and academia is essential to developing and maintaining space security. Specific intelligence related partnerships within those communities focus on data sharing and collaboration on analytical processes and methods. In order to establish and maintain these partnerships with other members of the IC, Guardians assigned to these organizations help fulfill Space Force and IC missions.

a. **The Intelligence Community.** The IC (figure 8) is a coalition of 18 US government agencies and organizations, led by the Office of the Director of National Intelligence (ODNI). The IC agencies fall within the Executive Branch, and work both independently and collaboratively to gather and analyze the intelligence necessary to conduct foreign relations and national security activities. The IC's mission is to provide timely, insightful, objective, and relevant intelligence to inform decisions on national security issues and events. The DNI executes the IC's mission including development of IC capabilities, information sharing and safeguarding, and partnering with domestic and international partners.

Figure 8. The intelligence community

As a member of the IC, the Space Force interfaces with the other members to collect, analyze, and share data relevant to the space domain and operations in all domains. Highlighted below are examples of specific interactions between the Space Force and other members of the IC.

1) **Office of the Director of National Intelligence (ODNI).** The Space Force intelligence enterprise receives funding from the ODNI's National Intelligence Program. The SF/S2 represents the Space Force at the DNI-led Intelligence Community Executive Committee, and other forums; supports and is supported by (as appropriate) the IC space executive and ODNI; and communicates Space Force intelligence enterprise science and technology needs to the ODNI-led National Intelligence Science and Technology Committee.

2) **Defense Intelligence Agency (DIA).** DIA's Missile and Space Intelligence Center (MSIC) is the DoD center of excellence for analysis and assessment of foreign air and missile defense systems, ballistic missiles, anti-tank guided missiles, anti-satellite missile systems, and directed energy weapons. MSIC expertise supports Guardians with evolving foreign space threat information.

3) **National Security Agency/Central Security Service (NSA/CSS).** NSA/CSS provides peacetime, contingency, crisis, and combat SIGINT and cybersecurity support to the US military, which includes supporting space intelligence operations. Guardians engage with NSA/CSS across the agency and key offices that influence space intelligence operations as members of the CSS. Delta 7 units embedded with NSA offices support space ISR mission sets. Other Deltas are embedded with NSA on a mission dependent basis. Along with the other military services cryptological offices at the NSA, the Space Force's Cryptologic Office, is the Space Force's primary staff agent for overseeing cryptologic operations, programming, budgeting, training, personnel, policy, doctrine, and foreign relationships.

4) **National Geospatial-Intelligence Agency (NGA).** NGA is the IC and DoD functional manager for GEOINT. Guardians work with NGA to develop an understanding of GEOINT detectable signatures for targets affecting space operations around the world. Delta 7 liaisons to NGA support the overhead persistent infrared missile warning mission.

5) **National Reconnaissance Office (NRO).** The NRO designs, builds, launches, and operates national reconnaissance spacecraft. It integrates unique and innovative space-based reconnaissance technology and the engineering, development, acquisition, and operation of space reconnaissance systems and related ISR activities. As a consumer of orbital and terrestrial counterspace, and cyber threat intelligence, the NRO is responsible for the integration and coordination of its requirements across the services as well as IC partners to support both its acquisition and operations missions, and as needed to execute its protect and defend mission. Guardians provide support for the NRO's space ISR mission sets.

6) **Army Intelligence.** The Army's National Ground Intelligence Center (NGIC) is the DoD's primary producer of ground forces intelligence. NGIC produces scientific and technical intelligence and military capabilities analysis on foreign ground forces required by warfighting commanders and the force modernization and research and development communities. The Space Force leverages NGIC expertise on foreign satellite communications (SATCOM) jammers.

7) **Air Force Intelligence.** The Air Force National Air and Space Intelligence Center (NASIC), in collaboration with NSIC (Delta 18), discovers and characterizes air, space, missile, and cyber threats to enable full-spectrum, all-domain operations, drive weapon system acquisition, and inform national defense policy.

8) **Naval Intelligence.** The Office of Naval Intelligence is the US military maritime intelligence service. NSIC (Delta 18) collaborates with the Office of Naval Intelligence to develop strategic intelligence relevant to the space and maritime domains. Office of Naval Intelligence products inform Delta 7 Guardians of maritime intelligence in the fulfillment of their own mission areas.

9) **Marine Corps Intelligence**. The Marine Corps Intelligence division under the deputy commandant for information exercise supervision over the Marine Corps Intelligence Activity (MCIA). MCIA has service responsibility for GEOINT, SIGINT, HUMINT and counterintelligence, and ensures there is a single synchronized strategy for the Marine Corps ISR enterprise. Space Force intelligence contributes to MCIA products supporting terrestrial operations.

b. **Joint Community.** Guardians assigned to the joint staff and each of the combatant command, as part of the Component Field Command (when established), provide space intelligence expertise and support to the mission of those commanders and their organizations. At the joint level, Guardians in the Joint Staff and National Military Command Center provide expertise in the areas of targeting, global warning intelligence, and current intelligence. Guardians at the combatant command's joint intelligence operations center (JIOC) support joint forces with space expertise for targeting, warning, and current intelligence. Guardians assigned to the USSPACECOM JIOC contribute to Commander USSPACECOM's responsibilities for space operations including global sensor manager, global SATCOM operations manager, space operations joint force provider, joint space operations training, navigation warfare operations and joint resilient positioning, navigation, and timing. Guardians assigned to USSPACECOM may also be part of the Joint Integrated Space Teams. Guardians assigned to the National Space Defense Center (NSDC) work alongside NRO, other members of the IC, and commercial partners to execute the protect and defend mission, deterring aggression, defending capabilities, and defeating adversaries throughout the competition continuum to maintain space superiority in the USSPACECOM area of responsibility.

c. **Inter-Agency Organizations.** The Space Force partners with US government organizations and agencies in developing space capabilities. One of those organizations is the National Aeronautics and Space Administration (NASA). NASA is an independent agency responsible for the civil space program, aeronautics research, and space research. Both parties are at current capability limits for extending SDA beyond GEO and addressing the need for near-Earth object detection and tracking. While the Space Force and NASA domains, missions, and operational cadence remain distinct and different, the benefits of shared technologies and observational data are of increasing interest to both communities. The Space Force partners with the Department of Commerce through a new memorandum of agreement for tracking of space objects. The Space Force also partners with National Oceanic and Atmospheric Administration (NOAA) for terrestrial environmental monitoring.

d. **Allies and Foreign Partners.** Strengthening our alliances, military partnerships, and security cooperation makes deterrence more credible and effective. Through these actions, military space forces can reinforce the confidence our allies and partner nations place in their relationship with the United States. As the space domain becomes increasingly congested and contested, developing and maturing key partnerships among our allies and partners becomes a critical enabler of space security. The Space Force continually reevaluates data sharing and collaboration agreements, including those for intelligence data, with its allies and partners.

e. **Commercial and Academic Partners**. The DoD and the IC are integrating data, analysis capabilities, and other services from commercial space entities and university programs. Remote sensing, surveillance and reconnaissance, geolocation, targeting, collection and analysis of radio frequency emissions, and electro-optical imagery from commercial space entities are enhancing DoD and space-based intelligence data.

Appendix A: Acronyms, Abbreviations, and Initialisms

ASAT	anti-satellite
C2	command and control
CHCSS	Chief, Central Security Service
CIA	Central Intelligence Agency
COMINT	communications intelligence
COMSPACEFOR	Commander, Space Force Forces
CSO	Chief of Space Operations
CSpOC	Combined Space Operations Center
CSS	Central Security Service
DCG-O	Deputy Commanding General for Operations
DIA	Defense Intelligence Agency
DIRNSA	Director, National Security Agency
DNI	Director of National Intelligence
DoD	Department of Defense
DoDD	Department of Defense Directive
ELINT	electronic intelligence
EMI	electromagnetic interference
EMP	electromagnetic pulse
FISINT	foreign-instrumentation signals intelligence
GEO	geosynchronous Earth orbit
GEOINT	geospatial intelligence
GPS	Global Positioning System
HEO	highly-elliptical orbit
HUMINT	human intelligence
IC	intelligence community
IMINT	imagery intelligence
IPOE	intelligence preparation of the operational environment
ISR	intelligence, surveillance, and reconnaissance
JIOC	joint intelligence operations center

KOT	key orbital trajectory
LEO	low Earth orbit
MASINT	measurement and signature intelligence
MCIA	Marine Corps Intelligence Activity
MEO	medium Earth orbit
MSIC	Missile and Space Intelligence Center
NASA	National Aeronautics and Space Administration
NASIC	National Air and Space Intelligence Center
NGA	National Geospatial-Intelligence Agency
NGIC	National Ground Intelligence Center
NOAA	National Oceanic and Atmospheric Administration
NRO	National Reconnaissance Office
NSA	National Security Agency
NSDC	National Space Defense Center
NSIC	National Space Intelligence Center
NUDET	nuclear detonation
OCSO	Office of the Chief of Space Operations
ODNI	Office of the Director of National Intelligence
OPELINT	operational electronic intelligence
OSINT	open-source intelligence
PNT	positioning, navigation, and timing
RFI	request for information
SATCOM	satellite communications
SDA	Space Development Agency
SDA	space domain awareness
SDP	Space Doctrine Publication
SIGINT	signals intelligence
SpOC	Space Operations Command
SpOC/CC	Commander, Space Operations Command
SpRCO	Space Rapid Capabilities Office
SSC	Space Systems Command
SSDP	Space Security and Defense Program
STARCOM	Space Training and Readiness Command

SWAC	Space Warfighting Analysis Center
TECHELINT	technical electronic intelligence
TECHINT	technical intelligence
TT&C	telemetry, tracking, and commanding
TTP	tactics, techniques, and procedures
U.S.	United States
US	United States
USAF	United States Air Force
USSF	United States Space Force
USSPACECOM	United States Space Command

Appendix B: Glossary

Collection. In intelligence usage, the acquisition of information and the provision of this information to processing elements. (Joint Publication 2-0)

Communications intelligence (COMINT). Technical information and intelligence derived from foreign communications by other than the intended recipients. (Joint Publication 2-0)

Decision advantage. The product of situational understanding, the ability to assure and exchange information, make, and communicate decisions by maintaining advantages in all domains. (Space Doctrine Publication 6-0)

Electromagnetic warfare. Military action involving the use of electromagnetic and directed energy to control the electromagnetic spectrum or to attack the enemy. (JP 3-85)

Electronic intelligence (ELINT). Technical and geolocation intelligence derived from foreign non-communications electromagnetic radiations emanating from other than nuclear detonations or radioactive sources. (Joint Publication 3-85)

Electromagnetic spectrum operations. Coordinated military actions to exploit, attack, protect, and manage the electromagnetic environment. (JP 3-85)

Foreign instrumentation signals intelligence (FISINT). A subcategory of signals intelligence consisting of technical information and intelligence derived from the intercept of foreign electromagnetic emissions associated with the testing and operational deployment of non-United States aerospace, surface, and subsurface systems. (Joint Publication 2-0)

Geospatial intelligence (GEOINT). The exploitation and analysis of imagery and geospatial information to describe, assess, and visually depict physical features and geographically referenced activities on the Earth. Geospatial intelligence consists of imagery, imagery intelligence (IMINT), and geospatial information. (Joint Publication 2-0)

Human intelligence (HUMINT). A category of intelligence derived from information collected and provided by human sources. (Joint Publication 2-0)

Imagery intelligence (IMINT). The technical, geographic, and intelligence information derived through the interpretation or analysis of imagery and collateral materials. (Joint Publication 2-0)

Information advantage. The superior position or condition derived from the ability to access, share, and collaborate securely via trusted information in order develop to more rapidly awareness and to execute decisions than an adversary while exploiting or denying an adversary's ability to do the same. (Space Doctrine Publication 6-0)

Information environment. The aggregate of individuals, organizations, and systems that collect, process, disseminate, or act on information. (Joint Publication 3-04)

Intelligence. 1. The product resulting from the collection, processing, integration, evaluation, analysis, and interpretation of available information concerning foreign nations, hostile or potentially hostile forces or elements, or areas of actual or potential operations. 2. The activities that result in the product. 3. The organizations engaged in such activities. (Joint Publication 2-0)

Intelligence asset. Any resource utilized by an intelligence organization for an operational support role. (Joint Publication 2-0)

Intelligence community (IC). All departments or agencies of a government that are concerned with intelligence activity, in either an oversight, managerial, support, or participatory role. (Joint Publication 2-0)

Intelligence discipline. A well-defined area of intelligence planning, collection, processing, exploitation, analysis, and reporting using a specific category of technical or human resources. (Joint Publication 2-0)

Intelligence, surveillance, and reconnaissance (ISR). 1. An integrated operations and intelligence activity that synchronizes and integrates the planning and operation of sensors, assets, and processing, exploitation, and dissemination systems in direct support of current and future operations. 2. The organizations or assets conducting such activities. (Joint Publication 2-0)

Key orbital trajectory. Any orbit from which a spacecraft can support users, collect information, defend other assets, or engage the adversary. (Space Capstone Publication, *Spacepower*)

Measurement and signature intelligence (MASINT). Information produced by quantitative and qualitative analysis of physical attributes of targets and events to characterize, locate, and identify targets and events, and derived from specialized, technically derived measurements of physical phenomena intrinsic to an object or event. (Joint Publication 2-0)

Open-source intelligence (OSINT). Relevant information derived from the systematic collection, processing, and analysis of publicly available information in response to known or anticipated intelligence requirements. (Joint Publication 2-0)

Signals intelligence (SIGINT). 1. A category of intelligence comprising either individually or in combination all communications intelligence, electronic intelligence, and foreign instrumentation signals intelligence, however transmitted. 2. Intelligence derived from communications, electronic, and foreign instrumentation signals. (Joint Publication 2-0)

Appendix C: Cornerstone Responsibilities, Core Competencies and Spacepower Disciplines

Cornerstone responsibilities. Military space forces conduct prompt and sustained space operations, accomplishing three cornerstone responsibilities. Taken together, these cornerstone responsibilities define the vital contributions of military spacepower. (Space Capstone Publication, *Spacepower*)

> **Preserve freedom of action.** Unfettered access to and freedom to operate in space is a vital national interest; it is the ability to accomplish all four components of national power – diplomatic, information, military, and economic – of a nation's implicit or explicit space strategy. Military space forces fundamentally exist to protect, defend, and preserve this freedom of action. (Space Capstone Publication, *Spacepower*)

> **Enable joint lethality and effectiveness.** Space capabilities strengthen operations in the other domains of warfare and reinforce every joint function – the United States does not project or employ power without space. At the same time, military space forces must rely on military operations in the other domains to protect and defend space freedom of action. Military space forces operate as part of the joint force across the entire conflict continuum in support of the full range of military operations. (Space Capstone Publication, *Spacepower*)

> **Provide independent options.** Providing the ability to achieve strategic effects independently is a central tenet of military spacepower. In this capacity, military spacepower is more than an adjunct to landpower, seapower, airpower, and cyberpower. Across the conflict continuum, military spacepower provides national leadership with independent military options that advance the nation's prosperity and security. Military space forces achieve national objectives by projecting power in, from, to space. (Space Capstone Publication, *Spacepower*)

Core competencies. The Space Force executes five core competencies. These core competencies represent the broad portfolio of capabilities military space forces need to provide successfully or efficiently to the Nation. (Space Capstone Publication, *Spacepower*)

> **Space security.** Space security establishes and promotes stable conditions for the safe and secure access to space activities for civil, commercial, intelligence community, and multinational partners. (Space Capstone Publication, *Spacepower*)

> **Combat power projection.** Combat power projection integrates defensive and offensive operations to maintain a desired level of freedom of action relative to an adversary. Combat power projection in concert with other competencies enhances freedom of action by deterring aggression or compelling an adversary to change behavior. (Space Capstone Publication, *Spacepower*

> **Space mobility and logistics.** Space mobility and logistics enables movement and support of military equipment and personnel in the space domain, from the space domain back to Earth, and to the space domain. (Space Capstone Publication, *Spacepower*)

Information mobility. Information mobility provides timely, rapid, and reliable collection and transportation of data across the range of military operations in support of tactical, operational, and strategic decision making. (Space Capstone Publication, *Spacepower*)

Space domain awareness. The timely, relevant, and actionable understanding of the operational environment. (*U.S. Space Force Vision for Space Domain Awareness*)

Spacepower disciplines. The spacepower disciplines are necessary components of military spacepower theory. These disciplines are the skills the Space Force needs when developing its personnel to become the masters of space warfare. (Space Capstone Publication, *Spacepower*)

Orbital warfare. Knowledge of orbital maneuver as well as offensive and defensive fires to preserve freedom of access to the domain. Skill to ensure United States and coalition space forces can continue to provide capability to the joint force while denying that same advantage to the adversary. (Space Capstone Publication, *Spacepower*)

Space electromagnetic warfare. Knowledge of spectrum awareness, maneuver within the spectrum, and non-kinetic fires within the spectrum to deny adversary use of vital links. Skill to manipulate physical access to communication pathways and awareness of how those pathways contribute to adversary advantage. (Space Capstone Publication, *Spacepower*)

Space battle management. Knowledge of how to orient to the space domain and skill in making decisions to preserve mission, deny adversary access, and ultimately ensure mission accomplishment. Ability to identify hostile actions and entities, conduct combat identification, target, and direct action in response to an evolving threat environment. (Space Capstone Publication, *Spacepower*)

Space access and sustainment. Knowledge of processes, support, and logistics required to maintain and prolong operations in the space domain. Ability to resource, apply, and leverage spacepower in, from, and to space. (Space Capstone Publication, *Spacepower*)

Military intelligence. Knowledge to conduct intelligence-led, threat-focused operations based on the insights. Ability to leverage the broader intelligence community to ensure military spacepower has the ISR capabilities needed to defend the space domain. (Space Capstone Publication, *Spacepower*)

Engineering and acquisition. Knowledge that ensures military spacepower has the best capabilities in the world to defend the space domain. Ability to form science, technology, and acquisition partnerships with other national security space organizations, commercial entities, allies, and academia to ensure the warfighters are properly equipped. (Space Capstone Publication, *Spacepower*

Cyber operations. Knowledge to defend the global networks upon which military spacepower is vitally dependent. Ability to employ cyber security and cyber defense of critical space networks and systems. Skill to employ future offensive capabilities. (Space Capstone Publication, *Spacepower*)

Appendix D: References

Space Capstone Publication, August 2020

Space Doctrine Publication 5-0, *Planning*, December 2021

Chief of Space Operations' Planning Guidance, 2020

U.S. Space Force Vision for Space Domain Awareness, May 2023

Joint Doctrine Note 2-19, *Competition Continuum*, June 2019

Joint Publication 2-0, *Joint Intelligence*, 26 May 2022

Joint Publication 3-0, *Joint Campaigns and Operations*, 18 June 2022

Joint Publication 3-04, *Information in Joint Operations*, 14 September 2022

Joint Publication 3-85, *Joint Electromagnetic Spectrum Operations*, 22 May 2020

Joint Guide for Joint Intelligence Preparation of the Operational Environment

DoDD 5100.20, *National Security Agency/Central Security Service (NSA/CSS)*, 26 January 2010

Intelligence Community Directive 203, *Analytical Standards*, 2 January 2015

Bate, Roger B, Mueller, Donald D., White, Jerry E. (1971). <u>Fundamentals of Astrodynamics,</u> Dover Publications Incorporated

Sellers, Jerry Jon. (2004). <u>Understanding Space: An Introduction to Astronautics</u>, McGraw Hill Publishing Incorporated

www.ingramcontent.com/pod-product-compliance
Lightning Source LLC
Chambersburg PA
CBHW080527110426
42742CB00017B/3264